Solo Guitar in Worship

by William Bay

To access the online audio recording go to:
WWW.MELBAY.COM/WBM80MEB

Exclusive Distributor: Mel Bay Publications, Inc.
WWW.MELBAY.COM

Preface

This is a collection of 25 guitar solos for use in Christian worship. Twenty-two are original solos and three are arrangements on sacred melodies from the 1500's and earlier. Most of the pieces are contemplative in nature. I have always been inspired and influenced by the following scripture text describing Elijah's encounter with the Lord.

> *"And he said, Go forth, and stand upon the mount before the LORD. And, behold, the LORD passed by, and a great and strong wind rent the mountains, and brake in pieces the rocks before the LORD; but the LORD was not in the wind: and after the wind an earthquake; but the LORD was not in the earthquake:*
>
> *And after the earthquake a fire; but the LORD was not in the fire: and after the fire a still small voice.*
>
> *1 Kings 19:11-12 KJV*

So these solos are, in general, written for those quiet, prayerful moments in worship where one can often feel the Lord's presence. I hope you enjoy playing and listening to these musical reflections.

William Bay

Contents

Holy Is the Lord

William Bay

Slowly and Freely

A

Guitar

Guitar

TAB

6

11

16

B

C
D
rubato

Canticle #1

Tenderly

William Bay

A

Guitar

mp

Guitar

B

dolce

C
rit.

Canticle #2

C
D
E

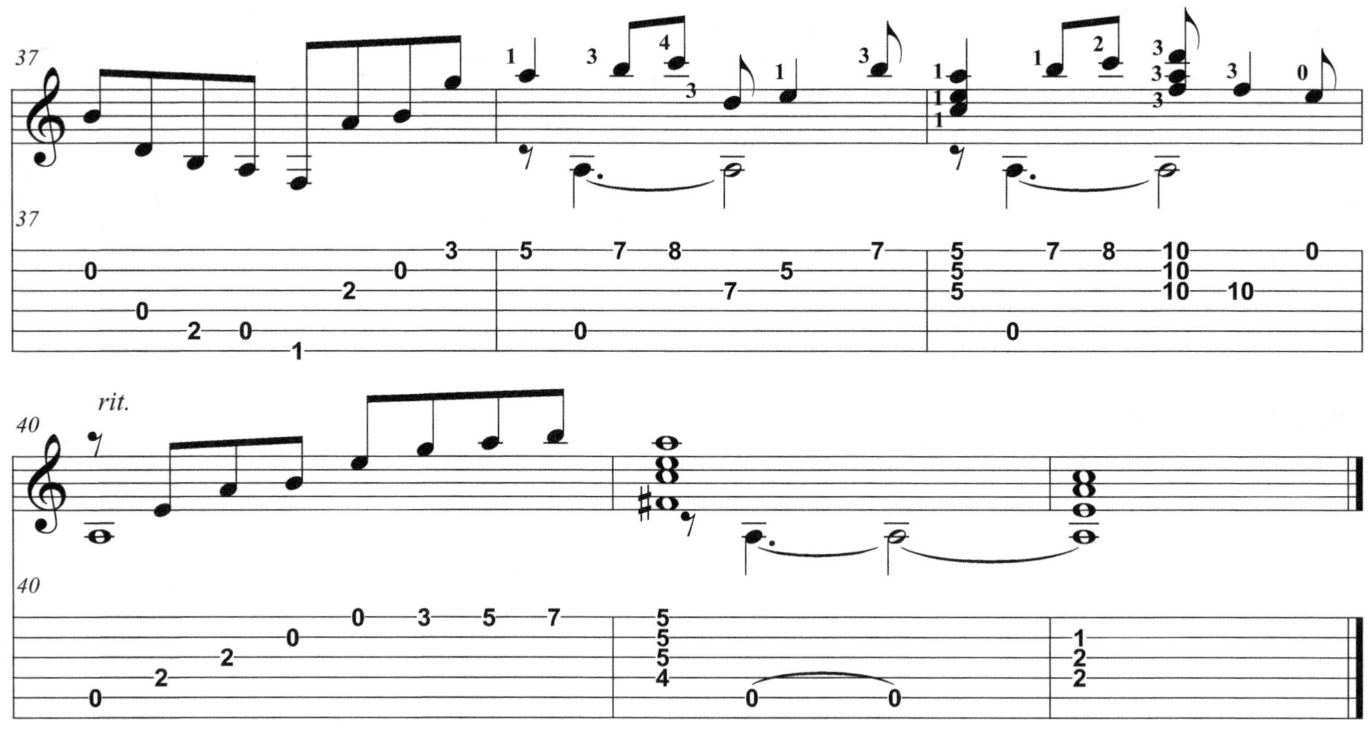
37
37
rit.
40
40

Adoro Devote

Dropped-D Tuning

Moderately Slow

13th Century Plainsong

Guitar

A

B

C

rit.

Kyrie Eleison

William Bay

Freely

A

Guitar

Guitar

T
A
B

5

5

B

9

13

13

C
D
rit.

Sanctus

Dropped-D Tuning

William Bay

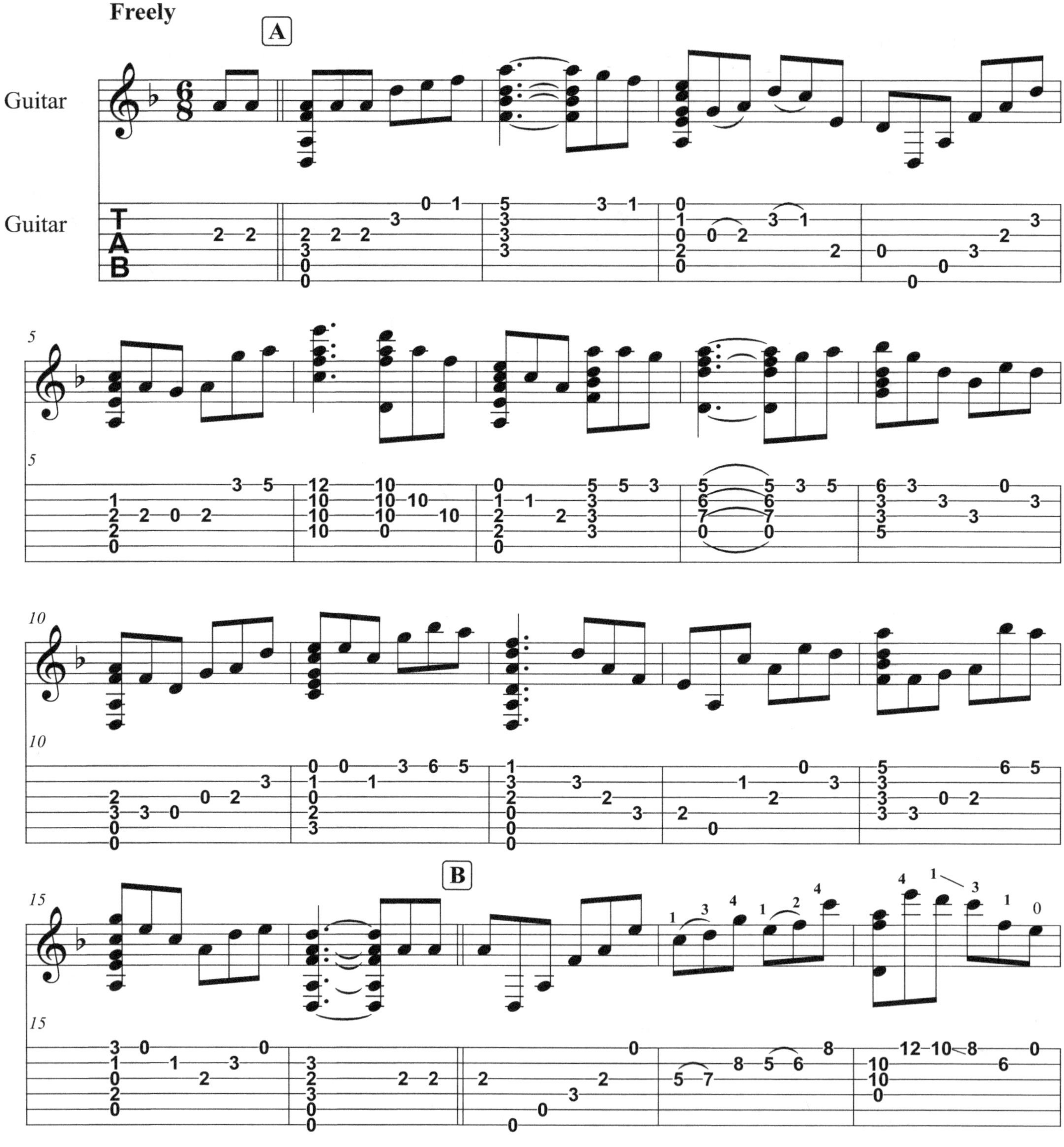

Freely

A

Guitar

Guitar

B

C
rit.
a tempo
rit.

Gloria
Jubilation

Joyfully

William Bay

A

Guitar

Guitar

6

6

11

B

11

16

16

C
D
E

rit.
F
a tempo
G

Prayer

C
D
E
p

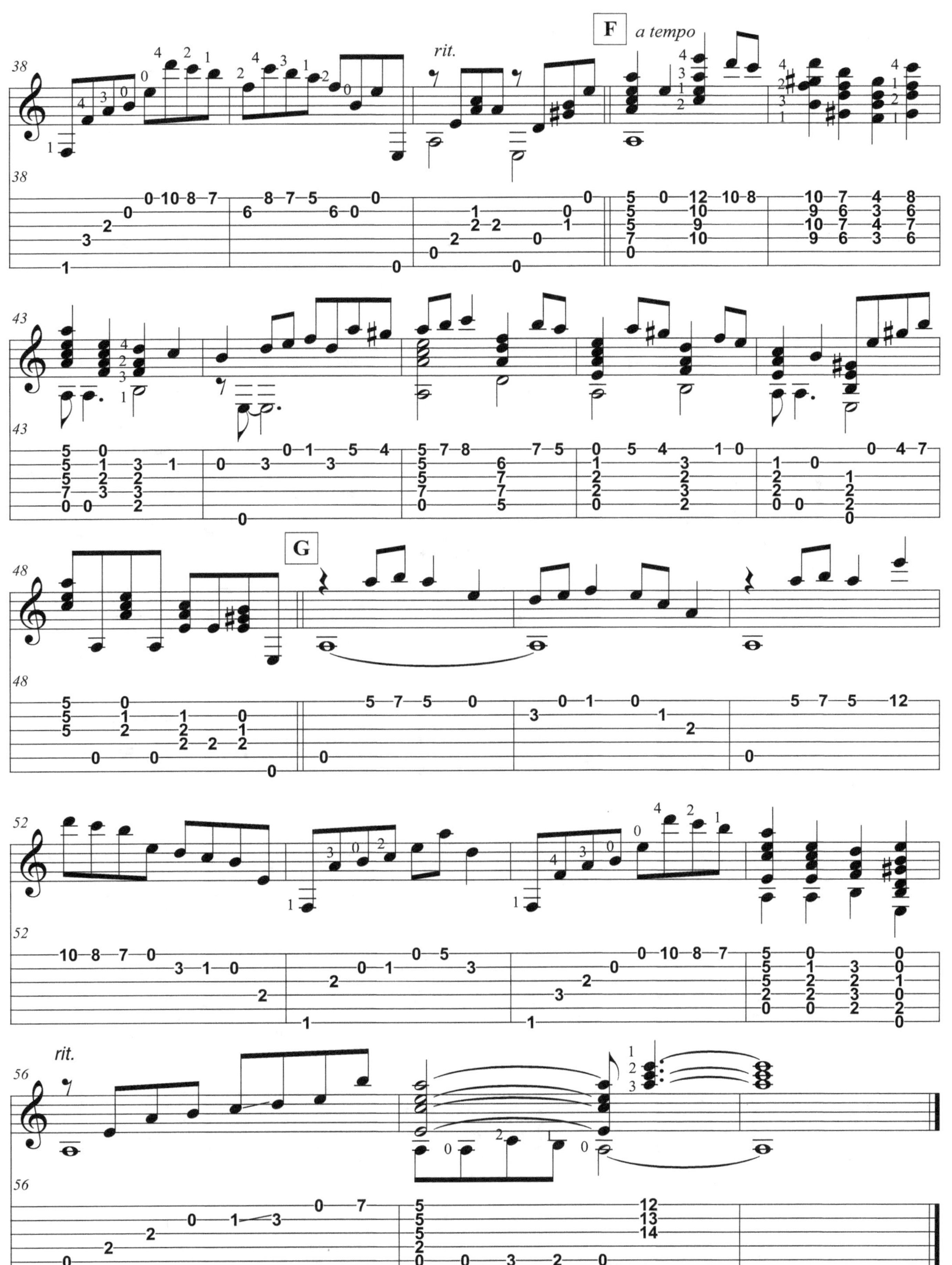
F
a tempo
rit.
G
rit.

Lamb of God
Agnus Dei

Adagio

William Bay

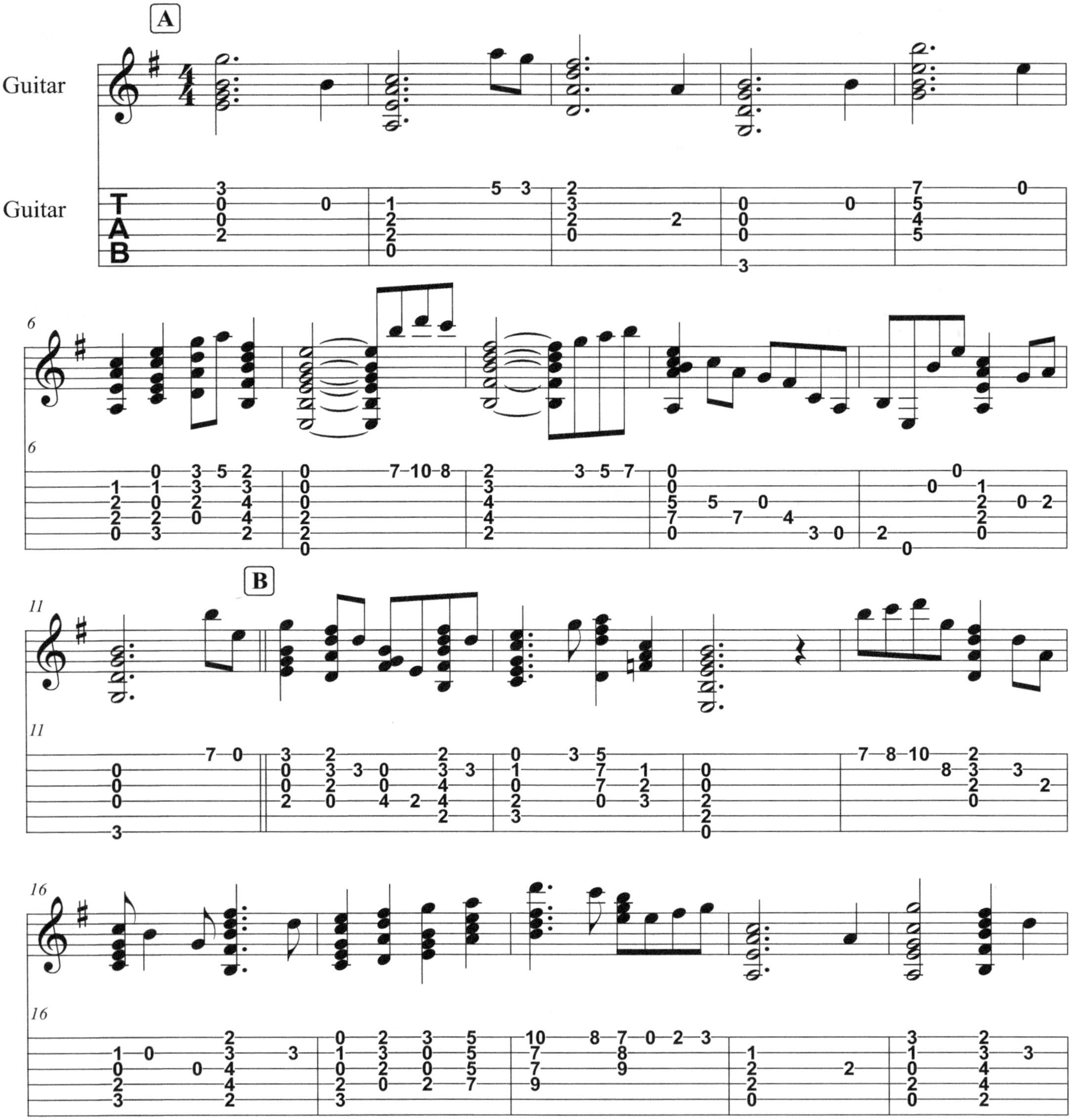

A

Guitar

Guitar

TAB

B

C

Come to the Feast

Moderato

William Bay

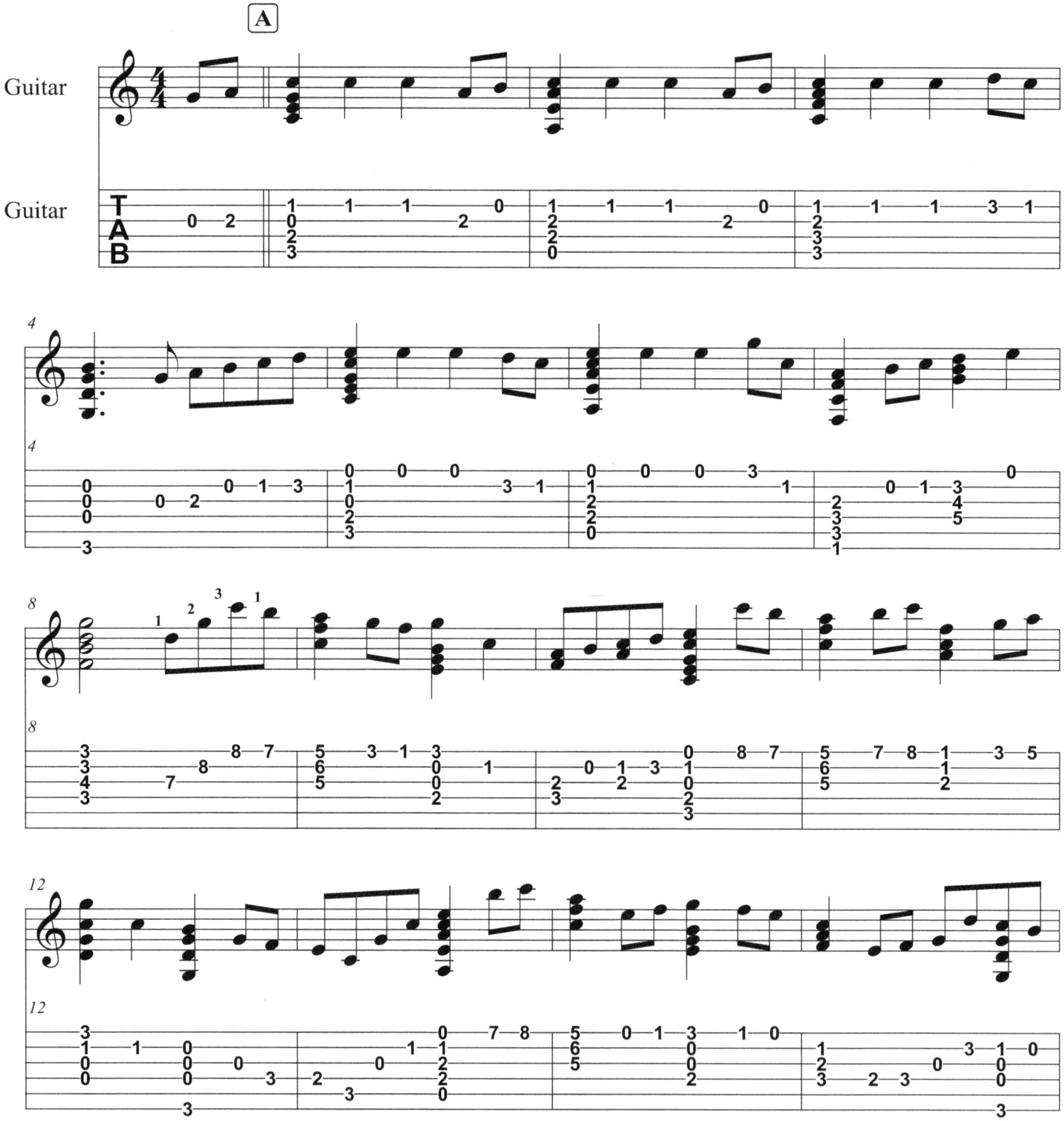

A

Guitar

Guitar

B
C
D

rit.

Peace

Dropped-D Tuning

Slow and Free

William Bay

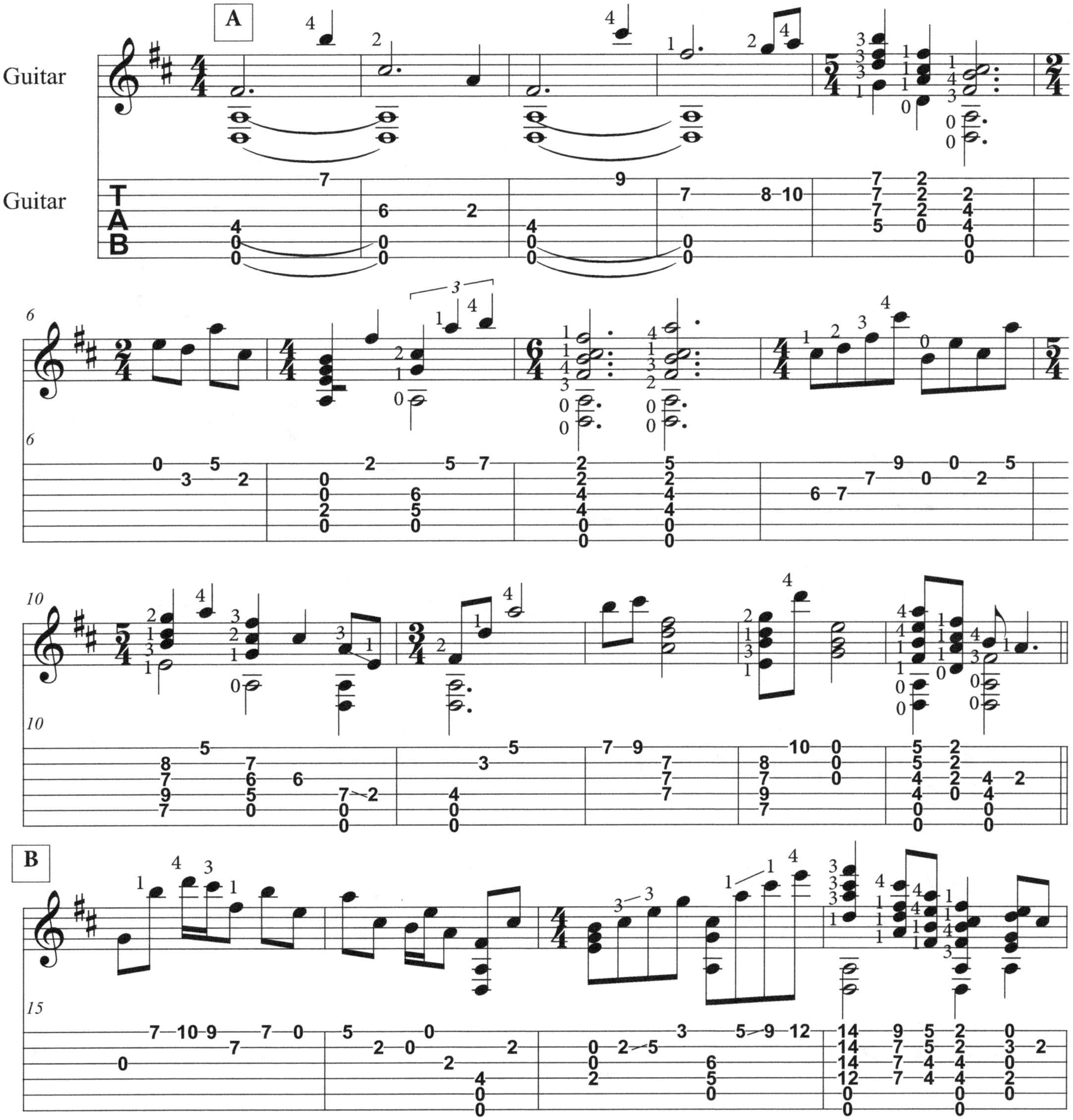

C

O Esca Viatorum

Gently

Louis Bourgeois 1549

A

Guitar

B

rit.

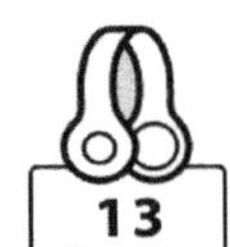

Rendez Á Dieu

Reverently

Louis Bourgeois 1543

A

Guitar

T
A
B

5

B

9

C

13

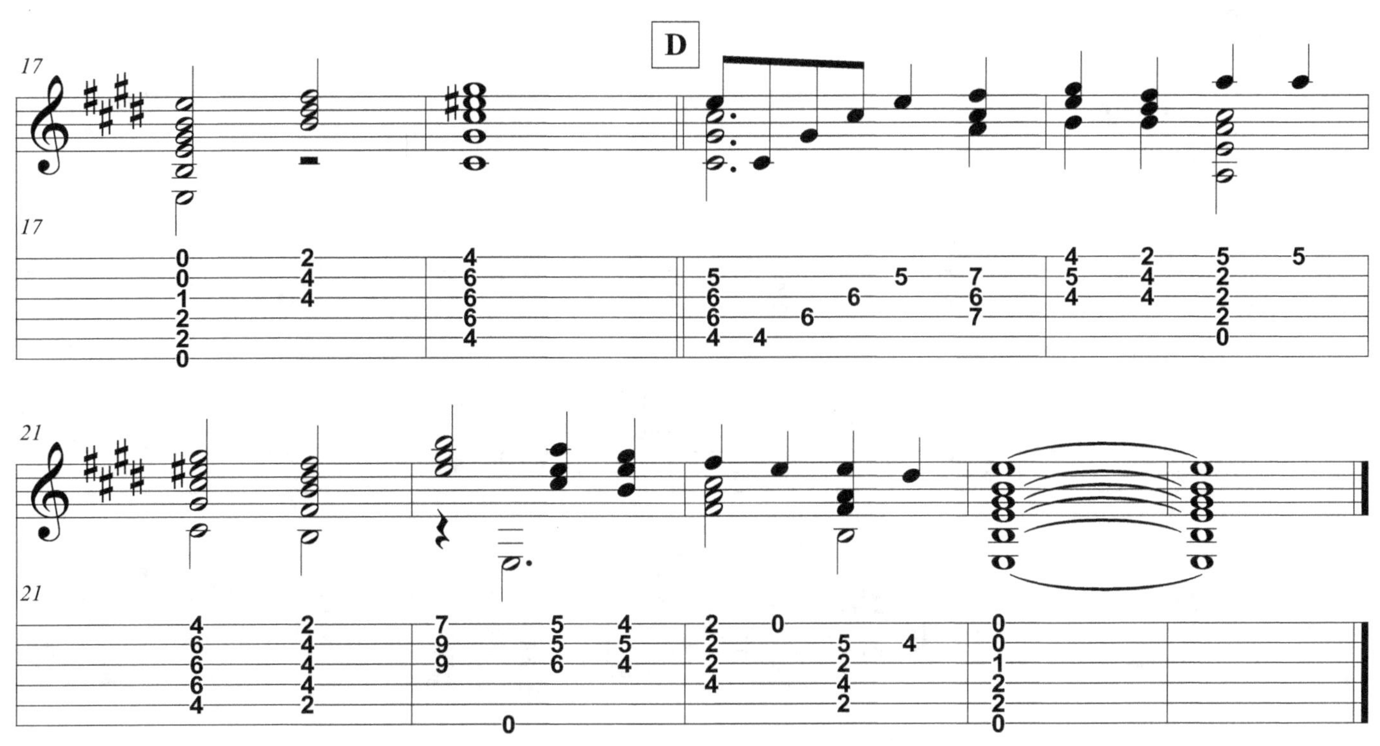
17
D
21

Light of the World

William Bay

Largo

A

Guitar

Guitar

8

8

B

13

16

16

C
D

Meditation on Psalm 13

Freely

William Bay

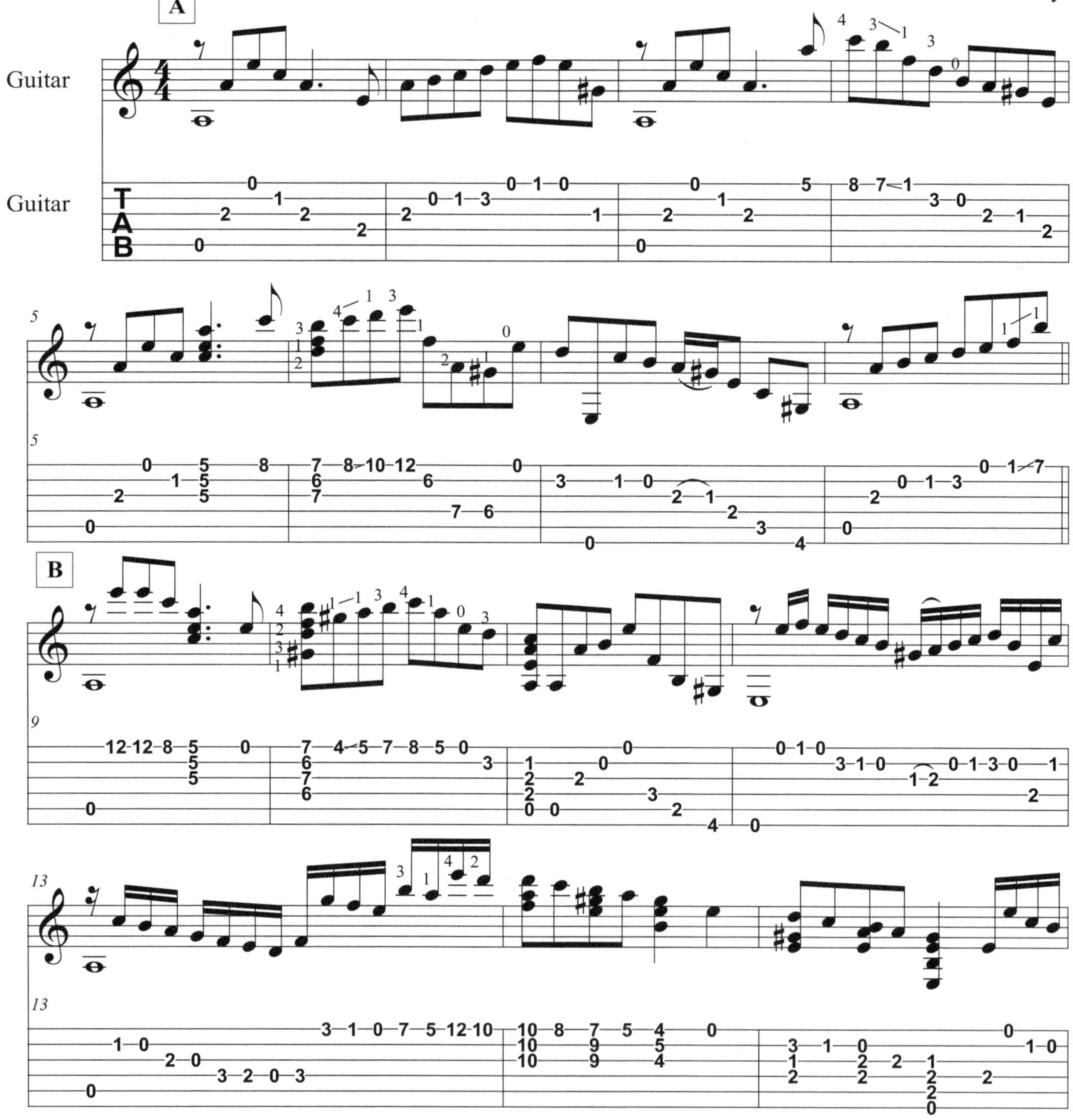

A

Guitar

Guitar

B

16
C
20
24
D
30
E
35

F
rit.
a tempo
G

51
55
58
rit.
H
61
67
I
mp
p

My Lord, My God

Adagio

William Bay

A

Guitar

Guitar

5

poco rit.

5

B *a tempo*

10

14

14

19
C
24
28
rit.
p

Lenten Meditation

17

Largo

William Bay

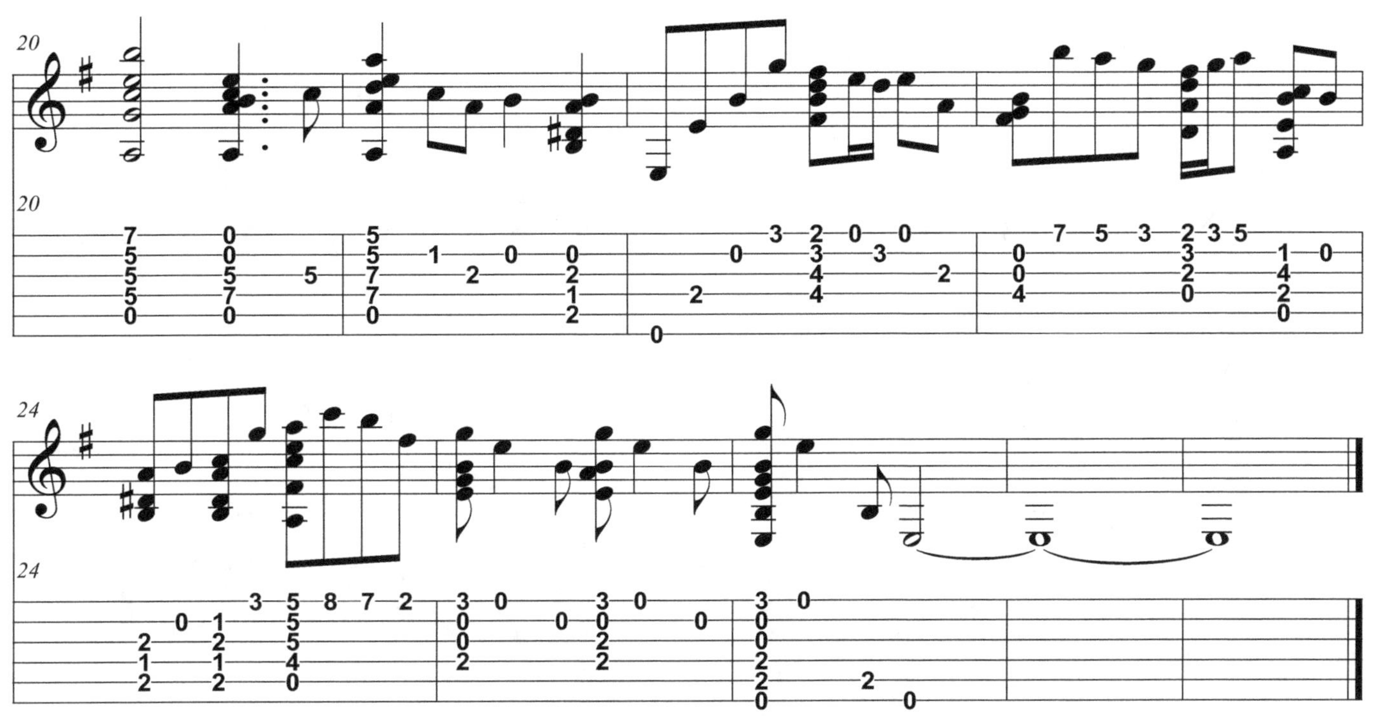
20
20
24
24

Litany

Gently

William Bay

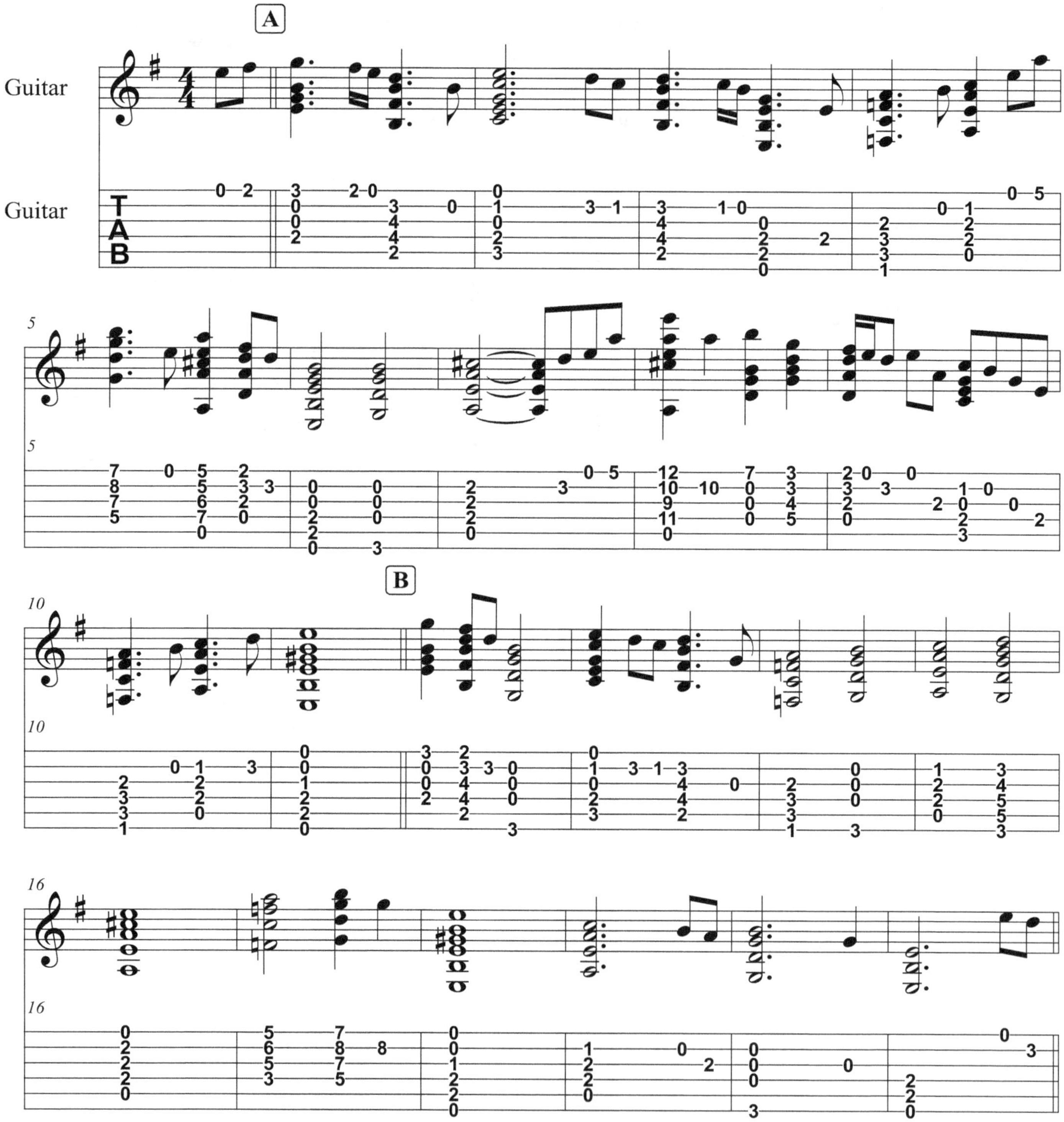

A

Guitar

Guitar

T
A
B

5

5

10

B

10

16

16

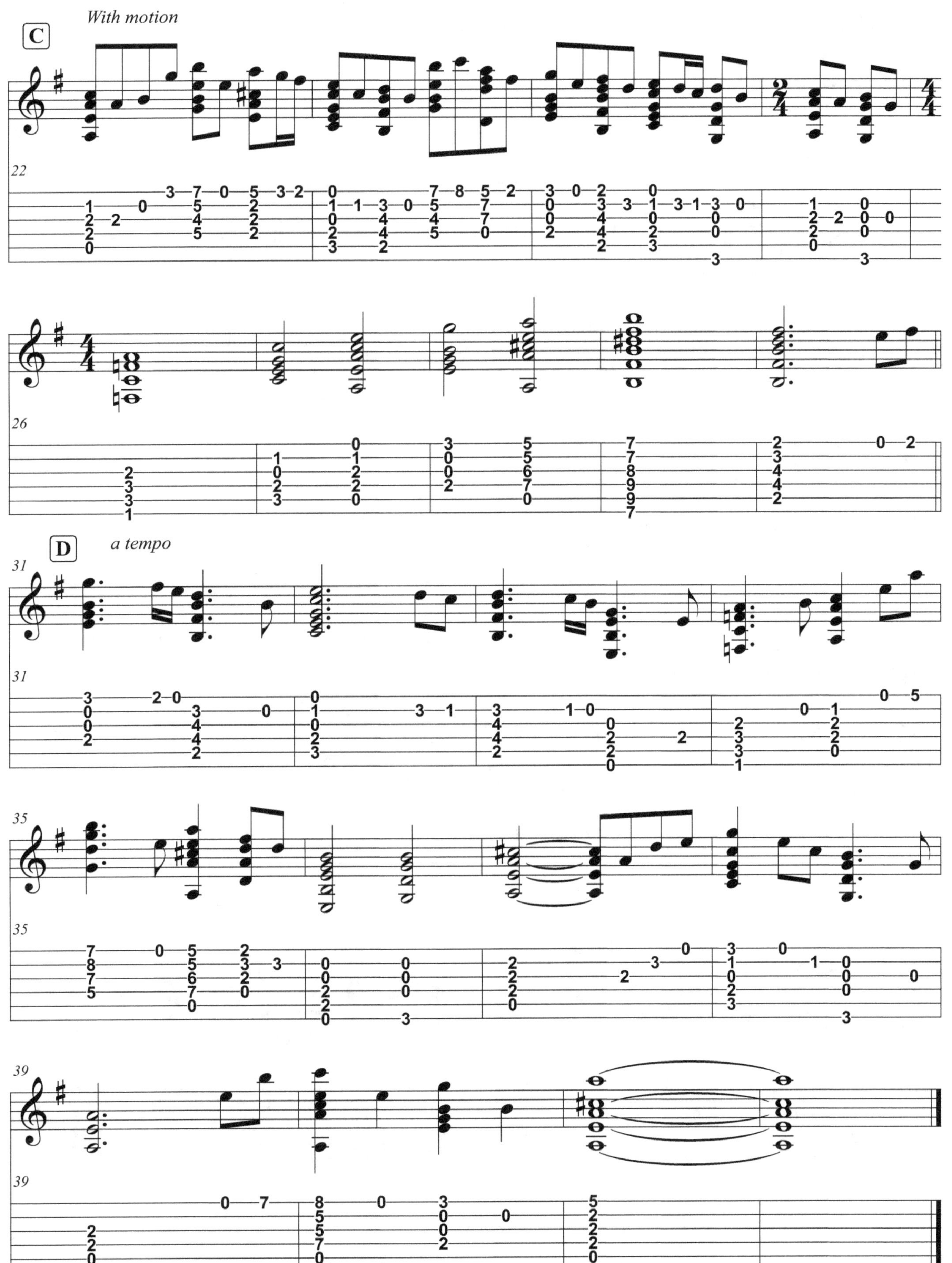

C
With motion
D
a tempo

Consecration

C
rit.
16
a tempo
20
rit.
20
D
a tempo
24
29
rit.
29

St. Gregory Chorale

Very Slow and Free

William Bay

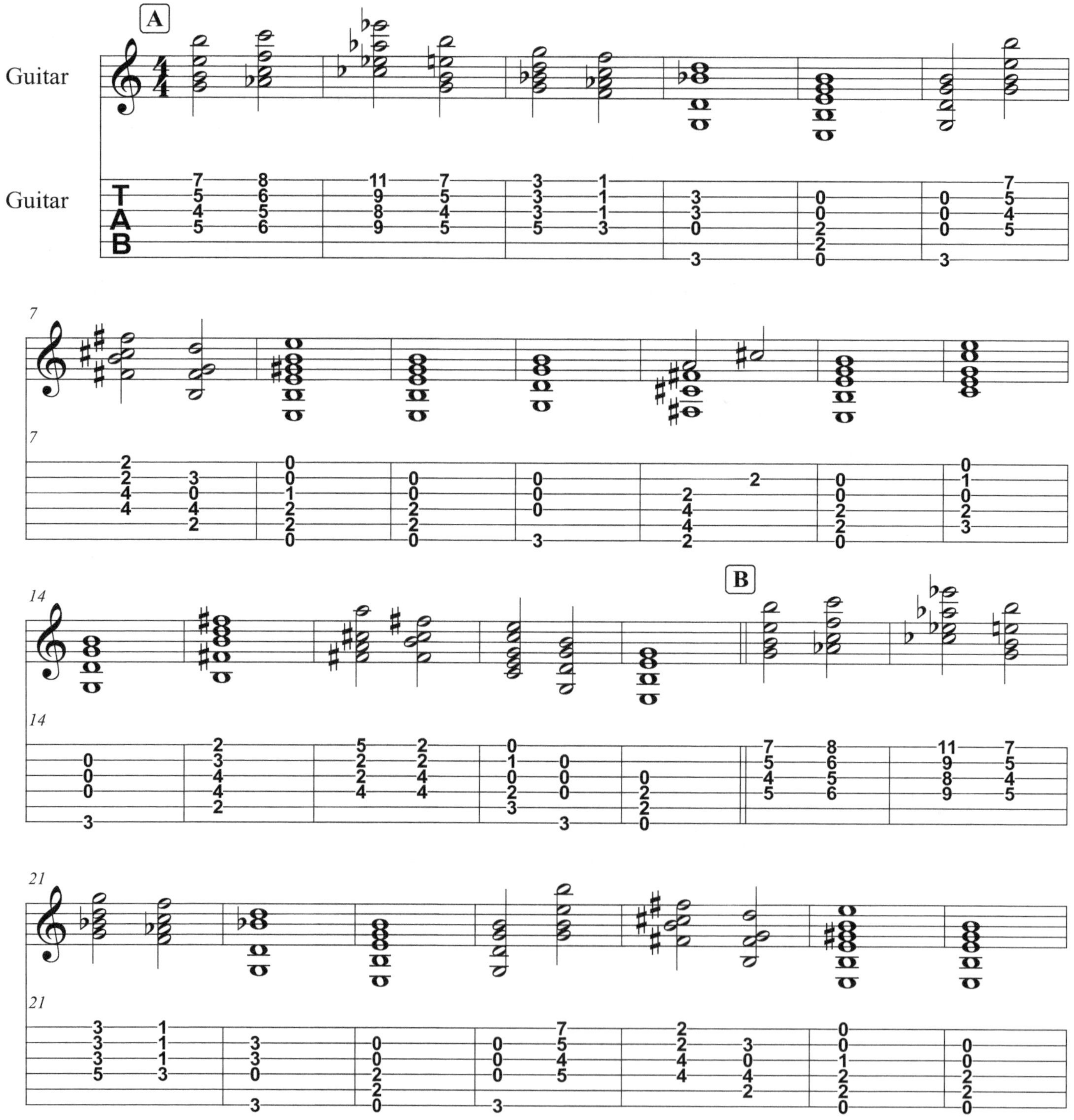

A

Guitar

Guitar

B

C
D

Evening Prayer

Gently

William Bay

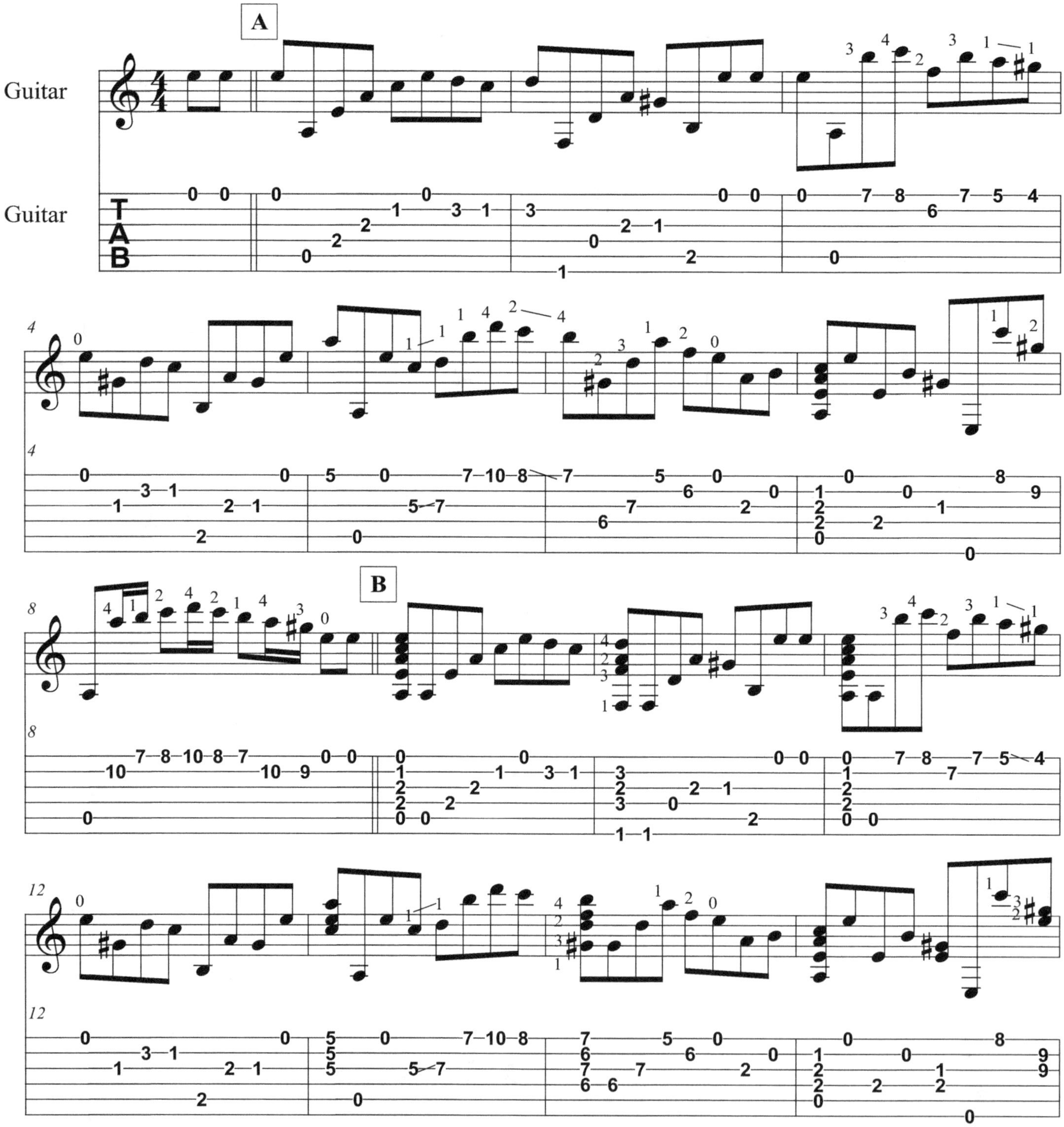

A

Guitar

Guitar

B

C
D
rit.
a tempo

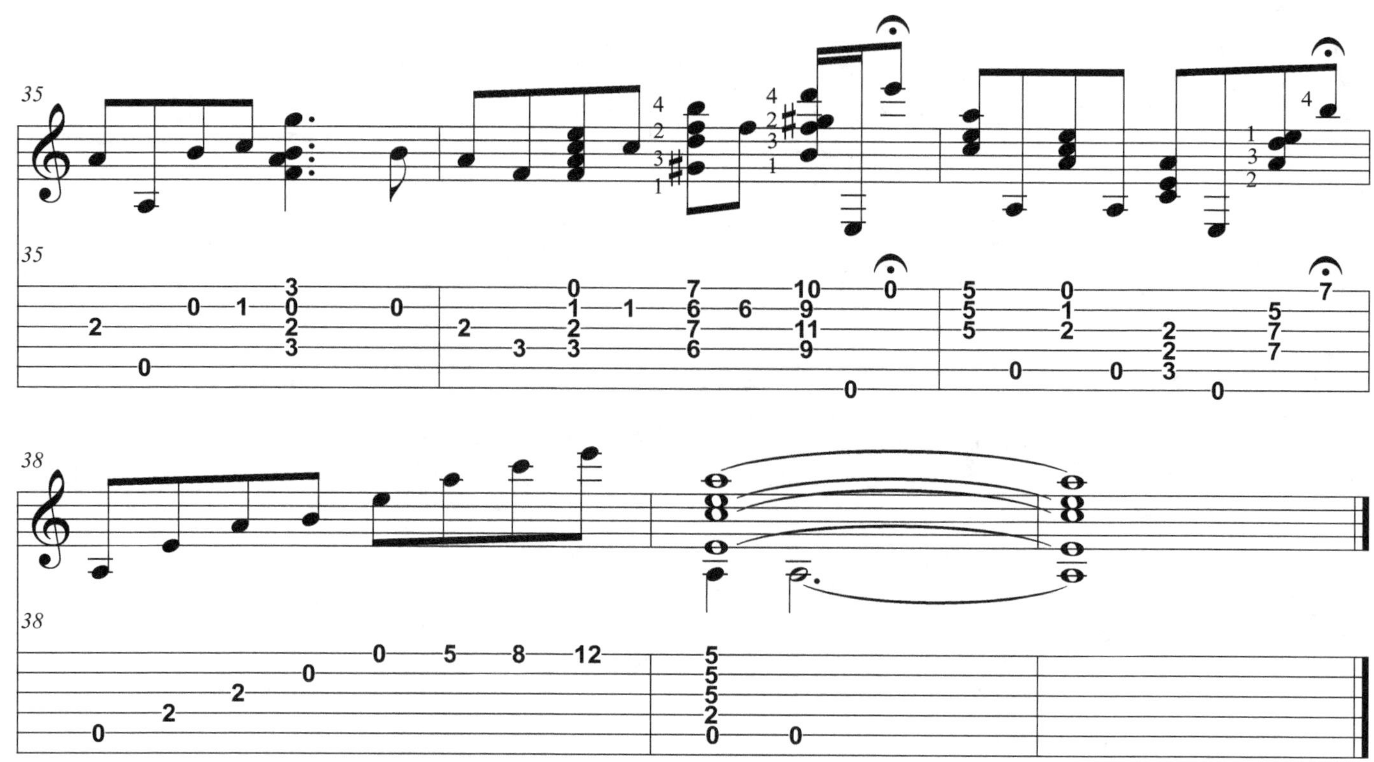
35
38

Prayer of Simeon

22

Nunc Dimittis

Lord, now let your servant depart in peace.

William Bay

C
rit.
a tempo
rit.
D
a tempo
E

rit.
F
rit.
G
rit.

Compline

Dropped-D Tuning

Gently

William Bay

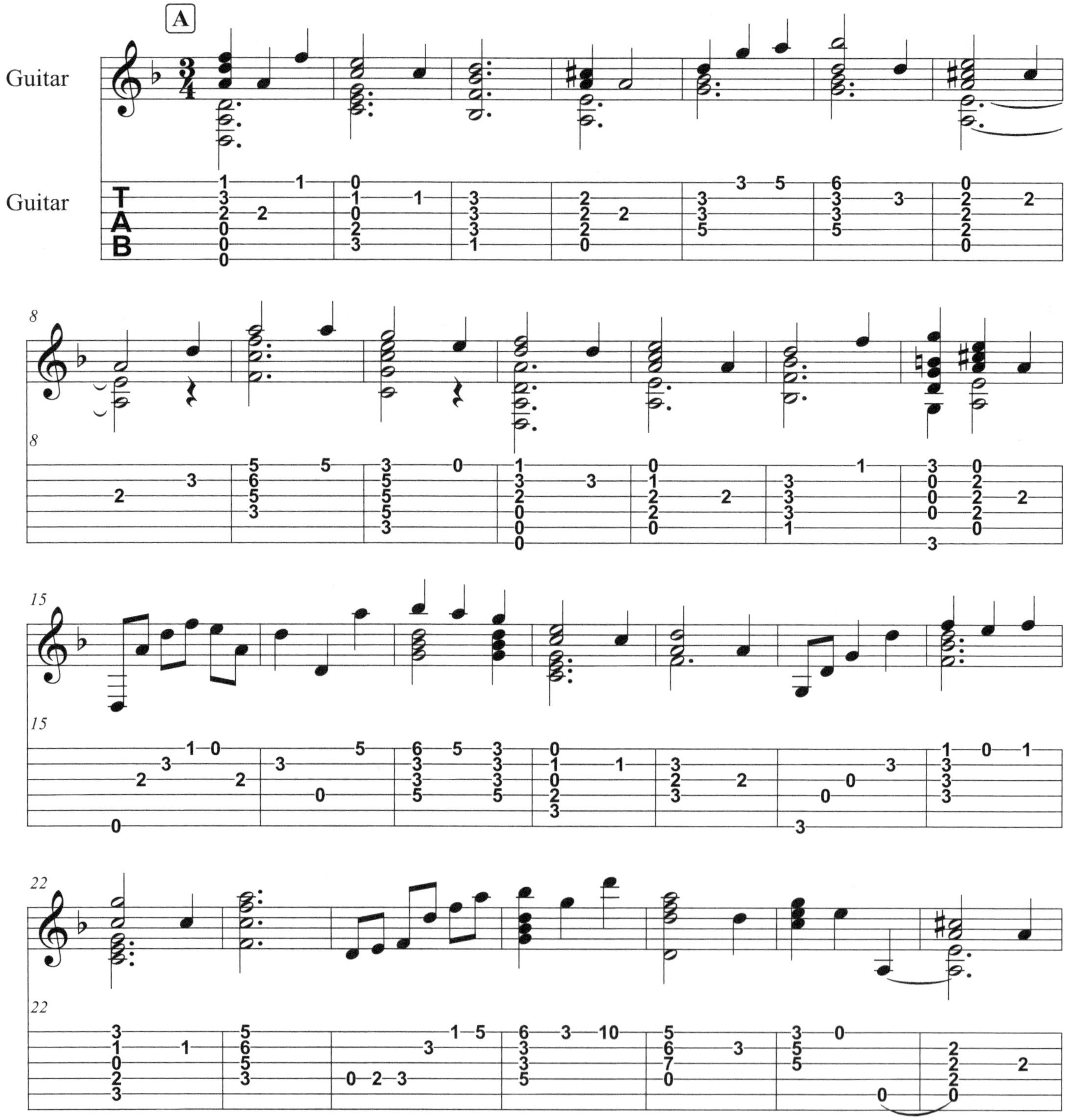

A

Guitar

Guitar

T
A
B

8

8

15

15

22

22

B
rit.

Night Prayer

Nocturne #3

Dropped-D Tuning

Slow and Free

William Bay

A

Guitar

Guitar

T
A
B

B

C
D
poco rit.
E

F
rit.
a tempo

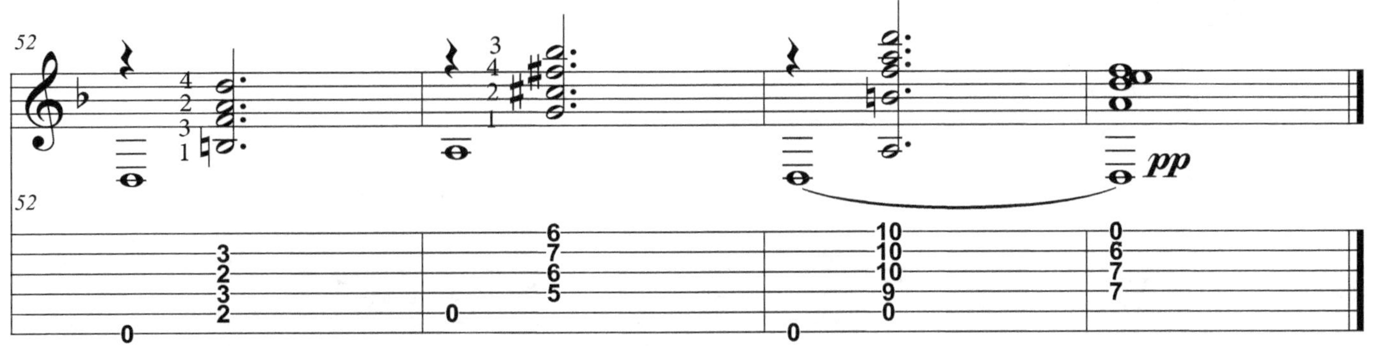
52
4
2
3
1
3
4
2
1
pp
52
3
2
3
2
0
6
7
6
5
0
10
10
10
9
0
0
0
6
7
7

Benediction

Dropped-D Tuning

Gently

William Bay

A

Guitar

mp

Guitar

T
A
B

mp

6

6

10

B

10

14

C

14

D

E
rit.

www.ingramcontent.com/pod-product-compliance
Lightning Source LLC
LaVergne TN
LVHW080557160826
845677LV00010B/1880

* 9 7 9 8 9 8 5 6 5 0 4 0 2 *